HOW TO
IMPROVE
SELF-ESTEEM
IN ANY
CHILD

IDA GREENE, PH.D.

Published in the United States of America

Brilliant Books Literary
137 Forest Park Lane Thomasville
North Carolina 27360 USA

ISBN:
Paperback: 979-8-88945-335-2
Ebook: 979-8-88945-336-9

Contents

Foreword

The book, *How to Improve Self-Esteem in Any Child,* poses questions and asks you to make drawings. This workbook is for you to write the answers and make the drawings.

Numbers in the box on most pages, e.g. $\boxed{\text{P 14.}}$, refer to relevant pages in *How to Improve Self-Esteem in Any Child.*

Chapter 1

Self-Esteem: The Essence of You

Your self-esteem is a blueprint of who you are, how you have been treated, respected, appreciated, and identified by those around you. Your self-esteem is endless; it is the essence of who you are, not what anyone may see you as. It is fragile. It can be affected by many factors and needs continual maintenance. It reflects how you view yourself; how you honor, respect, and value yourself. It paints a mental picture from your inner belief of who you think you can be, or what you believe you can do in your life

Five parts of our self-esteem

P. 14

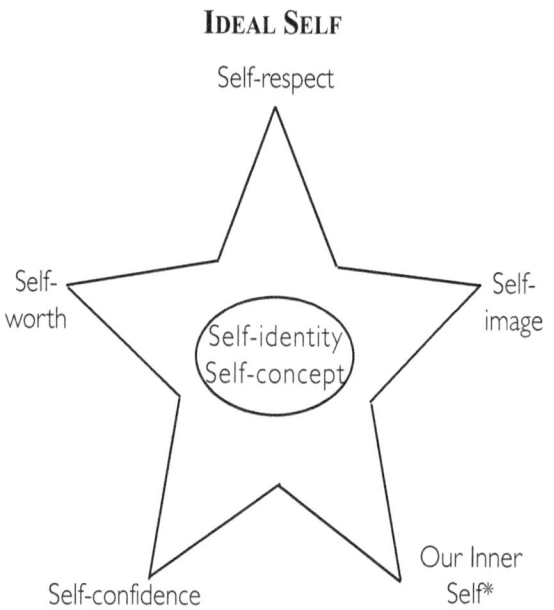

IDEAL SELF

Self-respect

Self-worth

Self-identity
Self-concept

Self-image

Self-confidence

Our Inner Self*

*The area of your Self that needs improvement for you to be a better person

2

Five parts of our self-esteem

P. 15

REAL SELF

Fill in the areas of the star where you are today

*Areas where you need to improve.
E.g., I avoid things,
I leave things undone,
I let my chores slide,
I do nothing at home/school.

Factors that negatively affect our self-confidence are:

P. 16

Shame (exclusion)
Over protection/concern
Hurtful words (hostility/blame)
Disapproval
Low expectations (little or no trust)
Ridicule
Fear

SELF-CONFIDENCE

To Have Self-Confidence You Need a "TAB"

1. **Think Confident**—With a "Can Do" Attitude
   a. Think "I can do it."
   b. Say, to yourself "I can handle this."
2. **Act Confident**
   a. Hold your head up
   b. Keep your shoulders back
   c. Sit tall in your seat
   d. Stand erect, with good posture
3. **Be Confident**
   a. Trust your divine (Spirit) self to show you the way
   b. Accept excellence as a way of life—Excellence has no fear of observation.
   c. Write down the things you believe that you do well.

   d. Write down the thing people say you do well.

Your self-esteem tells how you feel about yourself. The purpose of life and growing through relationships is, to refine your behavior, and learn more about yourself, so you become a better person.

4

YOUR SELF-CONCEPT/SELF IDENTITY

Is composed of:

* A THOUGHT is an unspoken word
* A WORD is a spoken thought
* Behavior is A THOUGHT AND WORD

Self-esteem is not a privilege. It is a right. However, children struggle on a daily basis to maintain their cultural identity, or sense of self. Children are open and loving; they lack the skills to nurture, protect, or maintain their sense of self against subtle, open bias, exclusivity, or rejection. Children must first like themselves, respect, and appreciate themselves before they can like another person

P. 21

STRENGTHENING MY CHARACTER

Answer the questions below.

1. What are your best qualities?

2. What talents do you have that other children/students don't have?

3. What talent/skills would you like, but don't have right now?

4. What qualities do you like the most in adults?

5. What qualities do you like the least in adults?

6. What qualities do you have that you want to change?

7. Would you like help or advice, to change a behavior or attitude? (Check one)

YES _____ NO _____
Ask Someone You Trust Today!

P. 20

This Is Me

Think of some adjectives that describe you. List one on each line below. Then number the adjectives from 1 to 6, using 1 to identify the quality you feel best about, 2 to indicate the one you feel next best about, and so on, down to 6.

Rating	Adjectives that describe me

P. 21

Now draw a line through the one you would most like to change. List below three things that you could do to change this quality .

1._____

2._____

3._____

Feelings and Emotions

P 23.

Choose 2 people you know — they could be family members, friends or even teachers. Draw one picture of what they look like when they're happy and another of when they're mad. Then circle which picture out of the two you like better.

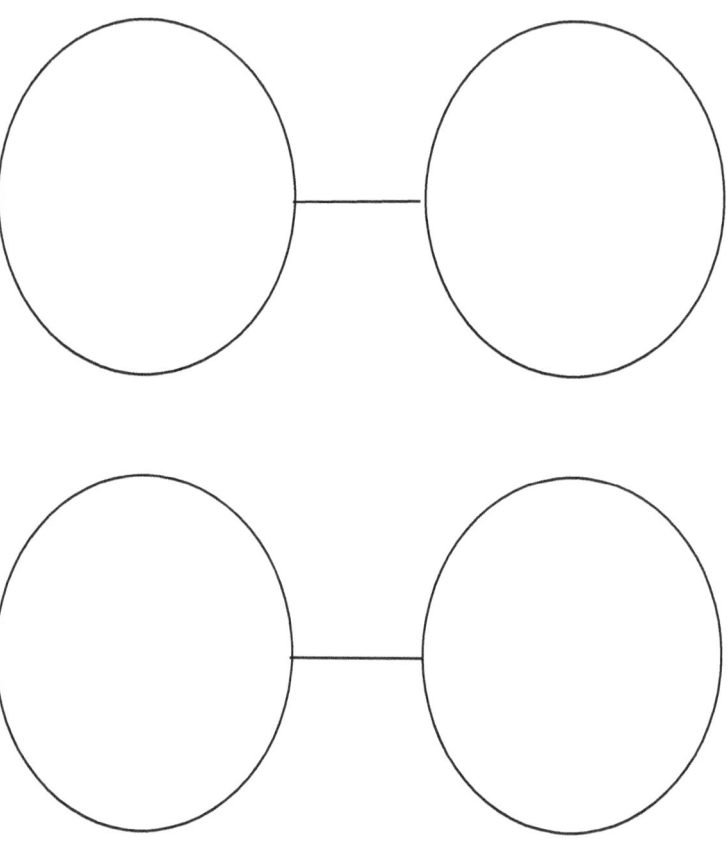

My Family Circle

P. 24

Draw yourself if the center circle and the rest of your family in the other circles. Then on the lines below, tell who helps you and how you would like each person in your family to help you.

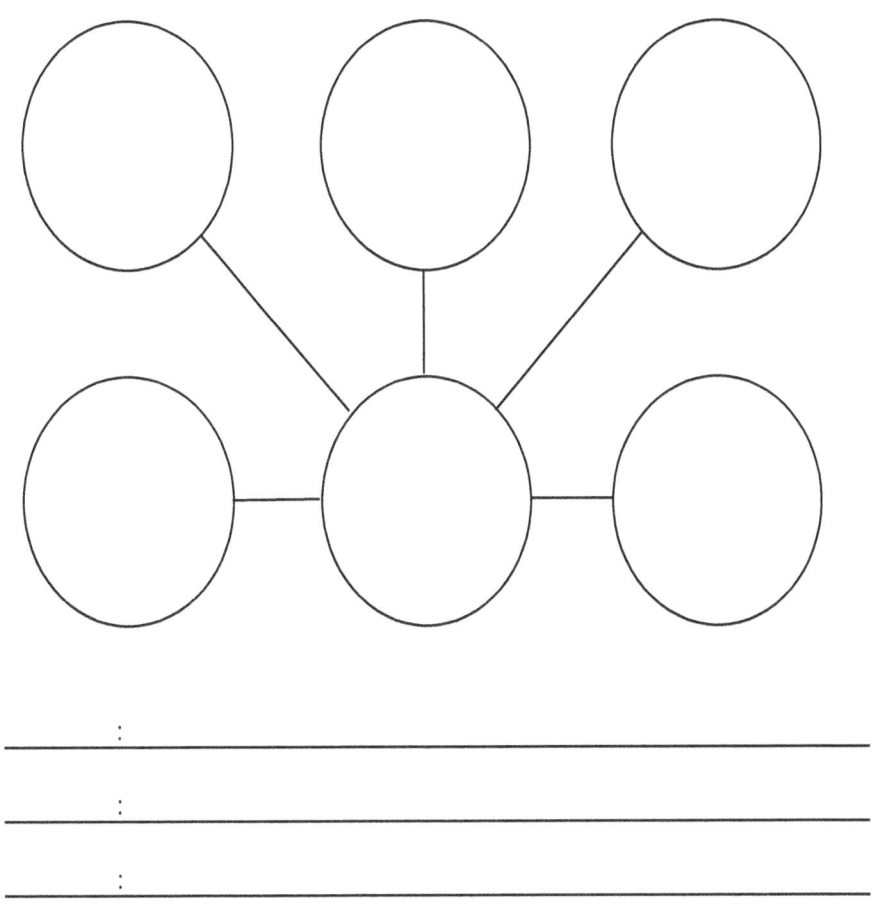

_____:_____

_____:_____

_____:_____

My Real Family

P. 25

In the spaces below, write 5 members of your family. Across from their name, tell what you like to do with that person.

Family Member
Example: Mom

What I like to do with them
Example: Play games, dance

1._____   1._____

_____

2._____   2._____

_____

3._____   3._____

_____

4._____   4._____

_____

5._____   5._____

_____

You Can Count On Me!

P. 26

We all count upon others for certain things. How do you count on these people and what do they count on you for? Complete the blanks below.

I count on Mom or Dad for	I count on my friend for
My Mom or Dad counts on me to	My friend counts on me for
I count on my teacher for	I count on my brother or sister for
My teacher counts on me to	He or she counts on me to

My Perfect Family

P. 27

If you could change your family, what would it look like? Draw yourself if the center circle and the rest of your ideal family in the other circles. Then on the lines below, write why you would like this person in your family.

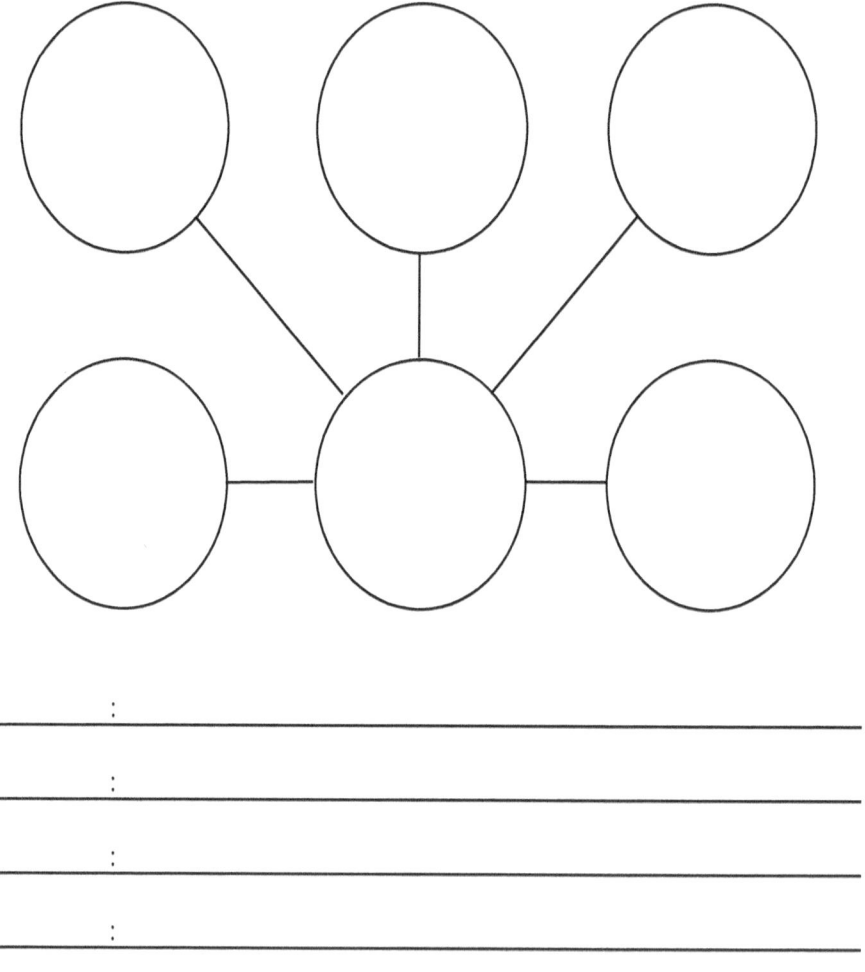

_____ :
_____ :
_____ :
_____ :

House Rules

P. 28

Answer the questions below.

1. What objects in your house are you not allowed
   to touch?

   _____

   _____

2. What happens if you touch something you're not allowed?

   _____

   _____

3. What things are you not allowed to do by
   yourself?

   _____

   _____

4. What things are you allowed to do by yourself?

   _____

   _____

5. Why do you think parents make these rules?

   a. _____

   _____

   b. _____

   _____

My Duties

In the spaces below list 4 duties you have at school and at home. Use the numbers below to indicate how dependable you are in doing your duties.

1 = poor
2 = fair
3 = good
4 = excellent

School Duties   Rating

1. _____   ___
2. _____   ___
3. _____   ___
4. _____   ___

Home Duties   Rating

1. _____   ___
2. _____   ___
3. _____   ___
4. _____   ___

14

Necessary Rules

Answer the questions below.

1. What would your house be like if you didn't have rules?

   _____

   _____

   _____

2. What would school be like if we didn't have rules?

   _____

   _____

   _____

3. If you were the teacher, what rules would you make for the class? List the 3 most important rules.

   a. _____

   b. _____

   c. _____

4. Would you make rules against hurting people's feelings? What would be a good rule?

   _____

   _____

   _____

5. What would be the punishment for breaking the rules?

   _____

   _____

The Classroom

P. 31

Answer the questions below.

1. In which ways is the classroom like a family?

   _____

   _____

2. What type of members of the family is there?
   Who is the parent?

   _____

   _____

3. List how a school is like a society.

   _____

   _____

   _____

4. If you were the ruler of the class, would you make it a dictatorship, democracy, or
   a monarchy?

   _____

   _____

   _____

My New Rules

P. 32

Answer the questions below.

1. What rules should be set for younger brothers and sisters to follow?

   _____

   _____

2. What rules should be set for older brothers and sisters to follow?

   _____

   _____

3. What new rules would you make for your family?

   _____

   _____

4. What new rules would you set for your school?

   _____

   _____

5. What new rules would you set for children and adults to follow?

   _____

   _____

6. If children and adults followed the same rules, what would it be like?

   _____

   _____

What I Wanted

P. 34

Everyone has wanted something special. Maybe you wanted a dog or a new game. Sometimes, when we don't get these things, we feel bad. Answer the questions below about what you felt like when you didn't get what you wanted.

The special thing I wanted was:	I wanted it because:
What did you want it for (Birthday, holidays, etc.)?	Whom did you want to do it?
Why didn't you get it?	Were you mad?

The next time I don't get what I want, instead of feeling mad, I'm going to:

_____

_____

_____

Chapter 2

The Beginning of You—
The Building Blocks of Self-Concept

YOUR SELF-CONCEPT HAS THREE SELVES:

P. 37

1. **A Personal Self-Identity/Self-Concept**: Your Expressive Creative self, is your ability to support yourself. It is your money-making ability. The Creative Self reflects your personal growth; it can be expressed through your desire for success or to achieve. It is your tendency to create your ideal self. It is an inner essence that is too often undiscovered, waiting to burst forth. Your Personal Self-Concept creates your daily circumstances through your thoughts, beliefs, and visions.

2. **Societal/Social Self**—Focuses on relationships and your interpersonal relationships. It changes to accommodate your social situation or environment.

3. **Spiritual/Self-Concept**—This divine part of you makes you reach out to help others. It is an expression of how you see yourself. It represents your undiscovered self and talents; it varies from situation to situation. Cultural values sometimes differ from societal values and cause confusion or conflict for an individual. For example, if a person's cultural value says it is O.K. to steal as long as you do not get caught, while the larger societal value says stealing is never an acceptable behavior, the discrepancy can cause confusion and uncertainty as to how you should behave. A person's cultural self-identity provides morals and values, and acts as a guideline for acceptable behavior.

KEY ELEMENTS OF YOUR CULTURAL SELF-IDENTITY

P. 39

Cultural Identity/Self-Concept → (moral, values) →
Ethnic Pride creates sense of belonging →
Self-Image → Self-Esteem =
1. Self-Worth
2. Self-Respect
3. Self-Confidence

Cultural Self-Concept/Identity—Your cultural self-identity provides morals and values and acts as a guideline for what are acceptable behaviors of conduct and manners. It is your identity as a member of a culture, or clan. It helps to formulate the self-concept. It is a point of reference about who one is, and where one comes from. Most cultures have a set of values of acceptable or appropriate behaviors a person is expected to display. Examples are:

- Cultural values of <u>acceptable behaviors</u>   P. 40
  1. Not speaking while another is speaking
  2. Asking before you touch the property of another
  3. Saying please, thank you

Write below:
- Cultural values of <u>unacceptable behaviors</u>
  1. Stealing—taking from others without their permission.
  2. Dishonesty—To distort or twist the truth
  3.
  4.

In the space below draw a picture of how you see yourself. Next to that picture draw how you would like to look or be, (This is your ideal self).

YOUR SELF-PERCEPTION

P. 46

List below four traits or qualities you would most like to have. Then state what you can do to gain these traits.

1.

2.

3.

4.

Finish this sentence: **I am special because**....

A.

B.

C.

Ethnic Pride is an important element of your cultural group. It gives you a sense of belonging. It gives distinction, or can be a source of embarrassment and disgrace. Some examples of Ethnic or Cultural Pride are:

1. Respect for elders (their wisdom and advice sought)
2. To not argue (talk back to adults)
3. Stealing—taking from others without their permission.
4. Dishonesty—telling an untruth (lie)

Can you think of other cultural values of unacceptable behavior? If so, list them below:

1.

2.

3.

In the space below, write the values your family or culture of origin feel are acceptable:

Finish this sentence **I Am Special Because...**

P. 48

    A.

    B.

    C.

WHERE DID I COME FROM?

Our culture provides an identity for us of how those who look like us began. It gives us a map to follow, and shows us how to begin. When the child is young, it seeks a point of reference as the beginning of self: Where did I come from? To whom do I belong? How did I get to earth? Are there other people who look like me? Our cultural ethnic identity answers this question. In the space below, fill in the blanks with the appropriate information about your family tree. Fill in the following blanks with the appropriate information about your family tree.

My name. . . . . Sex M/F . . . .

My birth date . . . . Birth weight . . . .

My birth place . . . . Time of birth. . . . .

Number of brothers . . . . Names . . . .

. . . .

. . . .

Number of sisters . . . . . Names . . . .

. . . .

. . . .

My favorite food/s . . . .

My favorite color/s . . . .

My favorite animal/pet . . . .

My Father's name . . . .

His birth date . . . . Birth weight . . . .

His birth place . . . . Time of birth. . . . .

Things I remember my father saying to me . . . .

. . . .

. . . .

Mother's name (married) . . . . P. 49
(maiden). . . . .

Her birth date. . . . . Birth weight . . . .

Her birth place. . . . . Time of birth. . . . .

Things I remember her saying to me. . . . .

. . . .

. . . .

Father's Mother's (My Grandmother's) **name** . . . .

. . . .

Her birth date. . . . . Birth weight . . . .

Her birth place. . . . . Time of birth. . . . .

Things I remember her saying to me. . . . .

. . . .

. . . .

Father's Father's (My Grandfather's) **name**. . . . .

. . . .

His birth date . . . . Birth weight

His birth place . . . . Time of birth. . . . .

Things I remember him saying to me . . . .

. . . .

. . . .

Mother's Mother's (My Grandmother's) **name** . . . .

. . . .

Her birth date. . . . . Birth weight . . . .

Her birth place. . . . . Time of birth. . . . .

Things I remember her saying to me. . . . .

. . . .

. . . .

Mother's Father's (My Grandfather's**) name** . . . .

. . . .

His birth date . . . . Birth weight . . . .

His birth place . . . . Time of birth . . . .

Things I remember him saying to me . . . .

. . . .

. . . .

Write any thoughts or feelings you have about your core family members. Which person has contributed positively to your self-esteem and self-confidence? What did they do?

P. 50

FACTORS THAT SHAPE OUR SELF-IDENTITY/
SELF-ESTEEM

There are many things that affect the person we are, and the person we present to the world. Are you aware that there are many different parts that make the whole you? You are composed of many thoughts, feelings, beliefs, attitudes, emotions, wishes, disappointments, dreams, and hopes.

Finish This Sentence: (Our culture gives us information about our ancestors, family members who lived before us.)

I am royalty because…

P. 51

A.

B.

24

Finish This Sentence:

P. 51

I am good at doing the following:
A.

B.

Self-Image. We don't always have an accurate picture of who we are. If any part that creates your self-image is distorted, your entire self-image will be distorted. To change a distorted self-image, you will need to change your self-concept. Improving your self-esteem requires you to improve your self-concept/identity, cultural identity, ethnic pride, and self-image.

These are key elements of your self-esteem that are essential for emotional maturity.

List below three behaviors you dislike about yourself. Put a check mark next to the one you are most likely to change.

• . . . . ☐

• . . . . ☐

• . . . . ☐

What steps can you take to make these changes?
List them.

1. . . . .

2. . . . .

3. . . . .

Factors That Lower Our Self-Esteem P. 53

- Self-limiting beliefs and negative thoughts
- Ridicule, embarrassment, shame, confusion, or hurtful words that make one feel badly.
- Lack of support from family members
- Acting out to gain attention
- Disrespect shown to yourself and others

What are some of the self-limiting beliefs, thoughts, orbehaviors that you see in yourself? List them.

- • . . . . ☐
- • . . . . ☐
- • . . . . ☐

A. Where did you hear these statements?

B. Write the name of someone who said something to you that made you feel bad about yourself.

Have you ever said any of the following statements to yourself? P. 54

a. I can't sing, dance, swim…
b. This is too much to hard for me to do
c. I don't like this/I hate doing this
d. I don't like her-him/I hate him-her
e. I can't finish this
f. This is boring, no fun, or stupid

C. Say the above statements aloud. Do you feel energized or tired?

How much feeling do you have to *Be*, or *Act Out* the above?

D. Listed below are some examples of positive beliefs/thoughts, attitudes, and behaviors:

a. This is easy
b. I can do this
c. This is fun
d. I am good at this
e. I am smart
f. Learning to do something new is exciting

E. Say the above statements aloud.
How do they make you feel?

Write your positive beliefs and/or thoughts below:

P. 55

F. Now it is your turn, write your positive, self-enhancing statements, and say them aloud to yourself.

a. I am intelligent
b. I figured "it out," I am smarter than I thought

c.

d.

e.

G. Which category of beliefs above has negatively affected your self-esteem? Write your answer below:

27

H. Has this influenced your home life or school
   performance?   Yes/No (Circle your answer.)

   How?

P. 56

I. What did you learn about yourself from the above exercises? Did you discover anything new about yourself? Yes/No (Circle your answer.)

This questionnaire will help you see how you feel about yourself.

Self Esteem Assessment

1. Who am I? I am....

2. Are you like your mom or dad? Is that good or bad?   P. 57

3. What makes you special/unique from others in your family or class?

4. What are your talents or gifts (things you do with ease that takes effort for others)?

5. What are your strengths and your weaknesses?

6. What makes your ancestry (family tree) special?

7. Ask yourself, "How do I lift myself up without putting who looks or acts different from me down?"

8. What can you do to communicate with others if you are shy or easily embarrassed?

9. Do you make friends easily with strangers?
    If your answers is "no", what can you do to overcome this obstacle?

10. How do you let someone know that you want to be his friend?

P. 61

THINGS THAT BLOCK GOOD FEELINGS ABOUT YOURSELF:

Confidence blockers are those feeling and situations that cause your confidence to melt away or decrease.

Confidence blockers are the uncertainties and insecurities we all feel in different areas of our lives...the fear of 'not measuring up'...the fear of not being who and what we like to be.

When does your confidence fizzle? What situations or feelings cause your confidence level to fall?

1. Being criticized?
2. Feeling out of place?
3. Personal rejection?
4. Feeling poor?

Overcoming confidence blockers requires positive actions that eliminate, or set off your loss of confidence caused by negative responses and uncomfortable situations.

The secret for overcoming confidence blockers lies in your ability to accept change. It is your ability to learn new skills or ideas.

The specific actions necessary to overcome your confidence blockers depend on you or the situation. Start today to change, *the only thing you have to lose is feeling lousy.*

Do any of these **confidence blockers** get you down? Remember identifying the **confidence blockers** is the first step toward getting rid of them.

CONFIDENCE BLOCKERS

P. 62

To <u>criticize</u> yourself or others.
To <u>complain</u> about yourself, your conditions, or others.
To <u>condemn</u> yourself or others, have a strong bias or prejudice for.

Are you guilty of saying or doing any of the above? Write comments below:
1.

2.

3.

P. 63

LIFE MIRRORS OUR BELIEF

What are your beliefs about yourself? Write your answers below:

The Following Is **True About Me**:	The Following Is **Not True About Me**:
1.	1.
2.	2.

My Self Perception

Think of words that describe you. Use words that tell others something about you. (E.g. friendly, pretty, etc.)
1.
2.
3.
4.
5.

EXERCISES TO INCREASE YOUR SELF-WORTH

Exercises to empower you and increase Self-Worth:
1. Write words you feel best describe you.

2. What words would others use to describe you? Why?

P. 64

3. Are you excited daily about getting up for school? Why?

4. What is/are your favorite food/s?
   Favorite car/s?
   What is your idea of fun?

TEENS 13-18 YEARS OLD

5. Why were you created?

   To do what?

   To be whom?

6. If you could live any place in the U.S. or world where would it be?

7. If you could do what you wanted, what would you be?

   If you could have what you wanted, what would it be?

   What would you do?

8. What do you think successful people do to become successful?

9. Will you go to college? Yes/No. Where?

Do you have enough happy times in your life?

Your thoughts control your life. And the question you ask yourself determines your happiness. Write five thoughts you are saying to yourself now. Are they happy or unhappy memories?

SELF-ESTEEM: THE ESSENCE OF YOU

P. 66

The key elements that negatively affect your self-esteem are:

Culture→Identity→Ethnic Pride→Acculturation→

Assimilation→Ridicule/Embarrassment→

Shame→Confusion→Feelings of Less Than

A. Which of the above category/ies have had a negative effect on the development of your self-esteem? Why?

B. State how this has influenced your personal life/school.

C. What thoughts do you have, that are not positive or uplifting?

THE BEGINNING OF YOU

To Light The Fire Within You™, learn how to be in control of your emotions and destructive urges. List ways you can avoid the following:

1. Resentment

2. Jealousy

3. Hostility

4. Rage

LIGHT THE FIRE WITHIN YOU™

Healing the Shattered Image

1. Have you forgiven your parents, childhood caretakers, or others who had the power to negatively influence your life? Write their names below.

2. What negative thoughts or attitudes do you have toward your parents?

3. These are ways I can develop my capacity to care and feel positive emotions towards myself:

33

4. I am learning to forgive and love myself and others who mistreated me in my childhood. Write the names of people you need to forgive. (e.g. sister, cousin, aunt.) What would you say to them?

P. 68

5. Shyness is caused by shame, embarrassment, or ridicule. What part of your self-image needs to be changed?

6. Write any negative thoughts or attitudes you have towards your parents/caretaker.

7. Are you able to forgive your parents, yourself, the Eternal Being? What can you do to heal this relationship?

8. List any thing that makes you feel sad, mad, anxious, or glad.

I feel sad when I think about:

I feel mad when I think about:

I feel anxious when I think of:

I feel glad when I think about:

9. What can you do to cope with feeling unloved?

P. 69

   A. Also learn to forgive anyone who has mistreated you. Can you think of anyone you need to forgive?

   B. List everyone below you need to forgive. Write a sentence to them. (E.g.: "Mom, I forgive you for not showing me love"; "Dad, I forgive you for ignoring/criticizing me.")

   C. Replace negative feelings about family members with positive ones.

   D. List things you can do to show love to yourself.

   E. Sit quietly, practice sending loving thoughts to yourself or others who have mistreated you.

35

10. Self-Confidence is a feeling of being self-assured or comfort with what you say or do. Can you think of an activity, or behavior you do, where you feel calm and self-assured?

P. 70

A. If not, what can you do to feel at ease with yourself when you perform in the presence of others?

B. Are your expectations of yourself realistic?

11. There are no two people alike. We were all created different.

A. Do you tell yourself you must be perfect to be an ok person.

B. Do you like yourself? Why? Why not?

C. Is there someone that you admire? Would you like to be more like that person? Why?

D. List below the thoughts/beliefs you have about yourself.

POSITIVE SELF-REGARD AFFIRMATIONS

P. 71

- I behave as an equal to all persons.
- I am smart.
- I am intelligent.
- I am knowledgeable.
- I am competent.
- I accept my goodness.
- I am perfect, just as I am.
- There is nothing I can do, say, think, or become that establishes my worth, my self-worth comes from the Infinite Spirit.

If I Could Change My Appearance...

P. 72

Some people aren't happy with the way they look and want to change a few things about themselves. Maybe you don't like the way your body looks or the size of your feet. Draw what you look like now in one box and in the other, draw what you want to look like.

Me Now   **How I Want to Be**

Trust Me!

P. 73

Answer the questions below.

Five people I trust are ,. . . . .

. . . . ,. . . . . ,

. . . . and. . . . .

I trust them because . . . .

. . . .

. . . .

. . . .

I think   (number) people trust me.

They trust me because

. . . .

. . . .

. . . .

I can earn other people's trust by . . . .

. . . .

. . . .

. . . .

A Glance Into the Future

P. 74

Complete the sentences below.

1. I want to become ....

   ....

2. When I graduate from college I would like to ....

   ....

   ....

3. When I'm an adult, I think I would like to ....

   ....

   ....

4. To be what I want to be when I'm an adult, I'll need to learn about

   ....

   ....

5. If I could change myself, I'd like to be more

   ....

   and less ....

   ....

6. If I could move to anywhere in the world, it would be ....

   ....

7. I would like to take these things or people with me when I move ....

   ....

   ....

40

10 Years From Now

P. 75

As people get older, a lot of things change about them. They may have a different hair color or a different job. Pretend that you are 10 years older and imagine what life would be like.

Draw a picture of what you think you would look like in 10 years and also write about how your ideas have changed since you were in school.

. . . .

. . . .

. . . .

. . . .

. . . .

. . . .

Chapter 3

How a Child Can Improve Their Self-Esteem

P. 77

Traditions are a useful way to impart knowledge from the past. On the continent of Africa, cultural traditions have a "Rites of Passage" ceremony which young boys and girls complete as they make the transition from childhood to woman/manhood. I have developed a modified program called "Life Skills Training" whereby young children ages 6-18 complete a 14-week series of structured classes, designed to help a child identify areas of their lives that need improvement or corrective action. The program is three-fold: covering the fourteen characteristics of high self-esteem, the Ten Commandments, and twelve values that should be mastered before reaching adulthood.

WHAT YOU CAN DO TO CHANGE YOUR SELF-CONFIDENCE

P. 83

You have control over and can change the following:

1. **Your Attitude**—It tells how you feel about yourself.

   a. Positive attitude builds self-confidence
   b. Negative attitude tears down self-confidence

2. **Your Environment**—The friends you choose reflect your self-image.

3. **Your Learning Skills**—Knowing how you receive and communicate information helps you learn faster.

   a. Visual Person—Learn through seeing
   b. Auditory Person—Learn through hearing
   c. Kinesthetic—Learn through moving, doing, and touch

Finish This Sentence: "I am special because…"

P. 83

    A.

    B.

    C.

To Know Your True Self, Answer These Questions

P. 86

1. Who am I?:

    I am…

2. What I really want to be/have in life is:

3. My likes and my dislikes:

4. Finish this statement, "I am most unhappy at home when I have to, need to:"

5. Finish this statement, "I am the happiest at home when I…"

Light the Fires Within™

P. 87

Self-Esteem, the Essence of You

To Discover Your Passion in Life, Ask Yourself These Questions:

1. What things in life give you the greatest pleasure or satisfaction? Write these down then put them in order of importance.

   Personal:

   Future Career Goals:

   Social:

   Spiritual:

2. What things do others praise or compliment you on?

3. Now that you have completed the activities above, what thing or things would you enjoy doing every day of the year, even if you were not paid with money?

SELF ESTEEM, ARE YOU READY TO CHANGE? P. 89

State how you can change the following:

1. **Your beliefs**—Core values about who you are.

2. **Your self-respect**—An appreciation of yourself.

3. **Your attitude**—The beliefs you have about yourself.

4. **Self-Image**—An inner picture of the person you desire to become.

5. **Self-Appreciation**—The acceptance of oneself; someone who knows their strengths and weaknesses; Someone who knows what they do well and where they need help.

6. How will you change self-defeating behaviors like procrastination, tardiness, or boredom?

7. To have more energy, to feel alive, and avoid

   the three Cs:

   P. 90

   - Criticizing

   - Complaining

   - Condemning

8. To experience more happiness, eliminate the following. Write what you will

   do to control or eliminate:

   a. Resentment

   b. Envy

   c. Jealousy

   d. Frustration→Irritations→Anger→Hostility→Rage

I will stop the cycle at the above point:

LIGHT THE FIRE WITHIN™

P. 92

Self-Esteem, the essence of you

1. Things I like about myself:

   Because..........

2. Things I dislike about myself:

   Because........

3. To Discover Your Strengths:
   List characteristics or traits that are uniquely you.

4. To find your weaknesses:
   List faults or areas of your personality you want to improve.

Secondary Factors That Affect Our Self-Esteem

1. **Listening Skills**—Hear new information, and decide to act or not to act.
2. **Shame**—Feel shy or self-conscious
3. **Rejection**—Lack of approval/self-dislike, low self-concept.
4. **Ridicule**—To feel blame or embarrassment with reason.
5. **Fear/Intimidation**—Anxiety about a real/imagined harm.
6. **Confusion**—Behavioral state caused by disapproval/rejection.
7. **Low/No Self-Respect**—No self-regard, inability to esteem self.
8. **"Something for Nothing" belief**—Allows one to be tricked, misled.
9. **Criticism**—Disapprove/fault find-Judge self and others.
10. **Lack of self-discipline**—No control over mouth, self-interest, antisocial behavior.
11. **Intolerance/Impatience**—Hot tempered, easy to anger/offend.
12. **Lack of Affection/Caring**—Inability to feel or express emotions.
13. **Lack of Security**—Inability to trust self or others.
14. **Lack of Encouragement or Praise**—Creates low self-worth.
15. **Low self-appreciation**—Unsure of self, harbor feelings of injustice, unfairness.
16. **Assimilate**—Integration into a group/culture that does not accept you.

P. 94

Write which of the above has affected your self-esteem, and what you will do to change this.

Ethnic Pride—is an important element provided by your cultural group. It gives you a sense of belonging, and acts as a point of reference. It can create a sense of distinction, or be a source of embarrassment and disgrace for you. This is especially true if your family member is a noted gang/drug leader, or is a relative of a respected public figure. You can use your ethnic pride as a tool to help you set goals, and feel proud of yourself. Acknowledging our heritage or culture gives us information about our ancestors, family members who lived long ago. Our culture gives us information about our ancestors, or family members who before you were born.

Complete this sentence, *I am royalty because…*

P. 100

Draw a picture of how you would look as a member of a royal family.

List some ethnic values of your family below:

P. 101

a.

b.

c.

Self-Image. Is an inner picture of how one see themselves, as reflected in their behavior. Our self-concept/identity is formed partly from our cultural identity through the morals and values shared with us by elders and the ethnic pride we develop. It creates a sense of belonging. From which we form our self-image.

MY SELF-ESTEEM

Using a scale of 0 through 10 (0 lowest, 5 average, 10 highest) choose the number that indicates how you feel at this moment and the number that indicate how you want to feel in each of the following areas of self-esteem.

P. 101

Self-Esteem Areas	I Feel	I Want to Feel
Sense of Uniqueness (Special+)		
Sense of Belonging		
Sense of Power		
Sense of Joy		
Sense of Wonder		
Sense of Integrity		
Sense of Mastery		
Sense of Purpose		

These are the areas of my self-esteem I choose to develop:

MY SELF-CONCEPT

P. 102

1. **Self-Concept/Identity**—Is it: nice person, poor me, be perfect, superiority-inferiority complex)? What mask/masks do you wear? How do you see yourself? List below:

2. Using your non-dominant hand, write about your self-concept.

P. 103

3. Using your non-dominant hand, draw a picture of your self-concept/self-identity.

4. Write one word that describes your self-concept/self-identity.

P. 103

5. What self-concept would you have if you were unhampered, or felt unlimited?

Draw a picture of this person.

P. 104

Blocks to your Self-Image and Self-Esteem

P. 105

1. Abuse-emotional/physical affects the total person.

2. Negative perceptions we hold about ourselves.

3. Negative perceptions others hold of us; the words they use when they describe us or the way they tease us; the way they treat us.

4. A mental image you hold of yourself. Is it a nagger, a complainer, stupid? What masks do you wear? How do you really see yourself? List below:

5. Write about your self-image. Your self-image is the outer picture of whoever you are inside.

6. Using your non-dominant hand, draw a picture of your self-image.

P. 106

7. Write one word that describes your self-image.

8. What self-image would you write about, if you were satisfied with yourself?

Through our desires and goals we become motivated to change our lives. To Discover Your True Self, Ask Yourself These **Questions:**

1. Who am I?:

P. 108

2. My likes are: My dislikes are:

3. I am good at:

4. What I really want to do in life is:

5. What/who is the most important thing/person in your life?

6. What is your goal in life?

7. What do you consider most urgent right now?

8. What has produced the most happiness in your life?

9. Finish this statement,

"As an adult, if I could only do one kind of work, it would be."

P. 110

10. "I am most unhappy when I have to,

or need to…"

11. Finish this statement,

"I am the happiest when I:"

12. "I am most unhappy at school when I

have to…"

13. "I am the happiest at school/home when I…"

Chapter 4

Agony and Ecstasy of the Evolving Self

P. 111

If you want to improve your self-esteem, you will have to change the way you think and act and the way you look at yourself.

If you are unhappy with yourself or your life you must take corrective action. This is a do it yourself task. No one can do it for you. Because no one knows your likes and dislikes. No one knows you intimately, but you andthe Great Spirit. And It knows you better than you know yourself. It knows who you are (his child), It knows who and what you are capable of being. The Spirit does not put limitations on your ability or your potential. It always says "Yes," to anything you want in life. The critical factors are that you want this with all your mind, body, and soul and that, you are willing to pay whatever price necessary to get what you want. You are unwavering in your desire or quest to have what you want, and most importantly—that it does not infringe upon the rights of your fellow human beings, and what you want is for the good of all people every where.

How To Help Others Get A Larger View Of Themselves

This exercise is a group project. Form a group of five persons. Each person should describe themselves to the group. As each group member describes themselves, make notes of each person's strengths, favorable characteristics they may have overlooked or not emphasized strongly. Take turns telling each person about your observations.

P. 116

1. Group member's name:......................................
   The favorable ways you impressed me were:

2. Group member's name:......................................
   The favorable ways you impressed me were:

3. Group member's name:......................................
   The favorable ways you impressed me were:

4. Group member's name:......................................
   The favorable ways you impressed me were:

5. Group member's name:......................................
   The favorable ways you impressed me were:

IMAGES OF YOU

If a child believes s/he will lose important relationships if s/he fails to meet others needs, or if s/he is different from others, s/he will develop a "public self" different from who the "private self" s/he is inside. Circle the words you think describes how other people perceive you now. Then put a box around the words you believe portray how you really are.

P. 118

How Others See Me

Angry	Insecure
Anxious	Intelligent
Attractive	Kind
Caring	Lonely
Confident	Sad
Considerate	Scared
Distant	Secure
Dumb	Sensitive
Fat	Skinny
Friendly	Soulful
Handsome	Tense
Happy	Warm
Inferior	

How I See Me

Angry	Insecure
Anxious	Intelligent
Attractive	Kind
Caring	Lonely
Confident	Sad
Considerate	Scared
Distant	Secure
Dumb	Sensitive
Fat	Skinny
Friendly	Soulful
Handsome	Tense
Happy	Warm
Inferior	

Chapter 5

Abuse—Its Effect Upon The Total Person P. 119

Emotional abuse affects our sense of self and self-esteem. An assault to our emotional health is equally as devastating as sexual or physical abuse because it injures the core of your personality.

You must be aware of this to insure you do not inflict the abuse you encountered and endured on others. This awareness is critical. We won't avoid doing something we don't consider a problem. We pass it on to the next generation.

Bad things do happen to good people. It is not what happens to you that matters, but how you feel, and react to what has happened to you. You can let a bad experience transform you to help others in a similar situation, or you can become bitter, angry, or rebellious, and unable to cope with life. Or you can work to forgive those who abused you, so you can live peacefully with yourself and others.

Abuse means mistreating another person. Abuse may be physical, emotional, or sexual. The word "abuse" can be used to mean each of these, or it can be used to mean all three of them.

Ways You Maintain Low Self-Esteem

P. 120

You Lower Your Self-Esteem By:

- ☐ Depending upon others for a sense of importance.
- ☐ Not accepting complete responsibility for your life.
- ☐ Depending upon others to do what you need to do.
- ☐ Not setting clear goals.
- ☐ Depending upon others permission before I am able to act.
- ☐ Not differentiating between who you are and what you do.
- ☐ Comparing yourself to others, to make them a gauge of your importance.
- ☐ Thinking your decisions need to be perfect or right.
- ☐ Failing to make choices, or think in a rigid/limited manner.
- ☐ Not giving yourself permission to make a mistake or fail.
- ☐ Not allowing yourself freedom to express your thoughts or feelings.
- ☐ Being fearful and anxious about things you can do nothing about.
- ☐ Thinking another person's brain is better equipped to solve your problems.
- ☐ Thinking you need to be perfect to be OK
- ☐ Being afraid to step outside your comfort zone or overly self-conscious.

Check the ones above that apply to you. Then explain, below, why this is an issue.

SELF-DESCRIPTION

P. 121

Answer these Questions for Yourself

Who am I? What am I like? How do others see me? What are my strengths? What are areas of my life I want to develop great skills in? Write a description of what you are like. This exercise will increase your self-awareness and communication skills. Sit down now, and summarize what you have learned about yourself.

1.

2.

3.

4.

Ways to Change a Low Self-Image

P. 122

1. Change all negative images you hold about yourself to positive.

2. Do you have negative thoughts, or feelings towards anyone? Who is it? Why?

3. What can you do to heal this/these relationship/s?

4. To know what you feel, write what you are feeling right now.

5. To cope with feelings of being unloved, list the names of anyone who has ever shown you tenderness or affection.

Chapter 6

Healing the Shattered Self-Image

HOW TO SET BOUNDARIES FOR YOURSELF

P. 123

Remember that you are a product of the wisdom, knowledge, genius, and cultural values of your ancestors, and people who lived before you. Who you are is the Eternal Being's gift to you. What you make of yourself is your gift to It. Will you give back to the Great Spirit the lump of clay from which you came? Or will your life be a masterpiece to behold? The answer is inside you. You hold the key to your future. You decide your destiny. You have been given the freedom of choice. You can make a difference. You matter and you are special. You have inside you all the talent of the ages. So walk tall and be proud. You are somebody.

How to Repair a Shattered Self-Image   P. 130

1. Have you forgiven your parents, childhood caretakers, or others who had power to negatively influence your life? Write their names below.

2. What negative thoughts or attitude do you have toward your parents?

3. Are you able to forgive your family? How can you heal this relationship?

4. List ways you can learn to care and show positive emotions for your parents or caretakers.

5. State ways you can forgive yourself, or those who have hurt you.

    A. List everyone below you feel hate for. What can you do to eliminate this feeling?

6. What parts of your self-image need improvement (self-worth positive self-regard/confidence)? What will you do about it?

7. List things you can do to show love to yourself

P. 131

8. Learning how to cope with feeling unloved?
   Do you feel no one cares for you? The Infinite Spirit cares for you.
   Write a letter to the Spirit in the space below:

Dear Great Spirit,

- Can you replace any negative feelings you have about yourself with positive feelings?

69

- List things you can do to show caring for yourself.

P. 132

- Sit quietly, practice sending love arrows to yourself or others who mistreated you.

9. Self-Confidence—A feeling of being self-assured, or comforted with what you say or do.
    - Can you think of an activity or behavior you do, where you feel self-assured?

    - If not, what can you do to feel at ease with yourself?

    - Are your expectations too high or unrealistic for yourself? Remember there are no two people alike. Everyone is different and unique. Are you angry that you are special?

    - Do you tell yourself you must be perfect to be an OK person?

    - Do you like yourself? Why? Why not?

- Is there someone you like better than yourself? Why?

P. 133

- List below thoughts you hold about yourself, good or bad.

How to Heal Old Hurts From Past Friendships P. 133

Answer the following questions in the spaces below.

1. How have your friendship(s) in the past affected your interactions with others. Are you able to see your faults?

2. Have you forgiven your parents, childhood caretakers, or others who had power to negatively influence your life? Write names of these persons.

3. What negative thoughts/attitudes do you have about your parents?

4. Things that block good feelings about yourself are:
   - Criticize yourself or others
   - Complain about yourself, your conditions, or others
   - Condemn yourself or others, a strong bias or prejudice

Can you change these habits? What will you do?

OTHER FACTORS THAT CREATE LOW SELF-ESTEEM

P. 135

1. Do you have a distorted self-image? Do you know what part/s of your self-image needs changing? Ask yourself if the self-image you now have is helping you reach your goals. Do you need to create a new image to match the new you? What can you do about this? Be specific.

2. Do you have envy towards or resent anyone?
   If so, it will hinder your success in life.
   If your answer is yes, write the names below.
   Daily, forgive these person for the harm they did to you.

3. Forgive parents/caretakers—What can you do to forgive your parents to heal the hurts of this relationship?

4. How to cope with feeling unloved—
   Learn to love yourself, then transfer that good feeling to others,

State How You Can Change The Following:

1. **Your beliefs**—What are your thoughts on what you will do with your life? Do you like yourself and other people?

2. **Self-Respect**—Do you behave in a way that makes you feel good about you?

3. **Your Attitude**—An attitude is negative behavior or feelings. Do you have negative feelings?

P. 136

   a. Why?

   b. Do you feel sorry for yourself?

4. **Self Image**—How can you change your self-image so it matches the person you want to be? What will you do?

5. **Self-Acceptance**—state what you will do to appreciate your *self* more.

6. **Negative Behavior**—What can you do to get rid of self-defeating behaviors like procrastination, tardiness, or boredom?

7. What can you do to control the following feelings: jealousy, resentment, anger, envy.

74

I feel jealous when I think about:

P. 138

I feel resentment when I think about:

I feel angry when I think of:

I feel envy when I think of:

8. Write other thoughts or feelings you have below....

,Draw what you feel as well.

Chapter 7

P. 141

Creating a Learning Environment to Improve Self-Esteem

I teach a twelve-week self-esteem class for African American students, coping with identity issues, behavior management problems or low self-worth. In one class, I gave the students four shapes: square, circle, triangle, and a squiggly shape and asked them to identify themselves with a symbol. 90% of the class saw themselves as squiggly. They were told later what the personality characteristics of each represented. The squares are organizers who plan things in advance, (mathematicians, scientists), circles are concerned about relationships-things working well together (teachers), triangles likes order and structure (accountants), and squiggles are creative, intuitive (musicians, artists, orally expressive).

Because of this mini survey, it was apparent to me that there was some cultural similarities. I wanted to be sure they accessed all areas of their brain, and utilized the seven kinds of intelligence that author, Thomas Armstrong mentions in his book, *7 Kinds Of Smarts*. He states, there are many ways to show intelligence.

The seven kinds of intelligence are:

1. Linguistic, the intelligence of words, this person can argue, persuade, or instruct through the spoken word.
2. Logical-Mathematical, the intelligence of numbers and logic, is the scientist, accountant, and computer programmer,
3. Spatial Intelligence involves thinking in pictures and images, the ability to perceive, transform and re-create different aspects of the visual spatial world (architects, pilots, mechanical engineers).
4. Bodily-Kinesthetic Intelligence of the physical self, includes talent in controlling one's body movements and handling objects skillfully (athletes, mechanics, surgeons).
5. Musical Intelligence is the capacity to perceive, appreciate, produce rhythms and melodies.

6. Interpersonal Intelligence is the ability to understand and work with other people (Dr. Martin Luther King Jr., negotiators, teachers).
7. Intra personal is intelligence, of the inner self. A person strong in this kind of smart can easily access her own feelings, discriminate between many different kinds of inner
emotional states and use her self-understanding to guide her life.

Examples of these individuals are counselors, theologians, self-employed business persons. Mr. Armstrong develops each of these intelligence's in his book, and gives excellent example of how to implement each. It would be wise for anyone who teaches African American children to be aware of the information in the book, *7 Kinds Of Smarts*. There are certain personality traits of the conditions conductive to learning required to maximize the learning experience, an ethnic minority child are listed below:

Personality Traits That Foster Learning: P. 143
1. Positive Attitude
2. Concentration
3. Being Focused (focusing of the eye span)
4. Erect Posture
5. Excitement for Learning
6. Desire To Be A Better Person
7. Drive To Know or Learn More
8. Have A Love Or Passion For Reading

Which of the above principles do you have, or now use at school or home? Write your thoughts or feelings about this now.

All children perceive the world in a different way, therefore they learn differently. Many are visual (sight) learners, others learn by auditory (hearing), while others learn or experience the world through kinesthetic (touch) sensation. Go through the statements below. Decide if the statement refers to someone who is a visual, auditory, or kinesthetic learner. Write A, V, or K in the box in front of the statement. Then write the word "me" in the box at the end of each statement that applies to you. Tally your responses to find the dominant channel you use to learn or express yourself.

P. 144

Learning Styles Inventory

A/V/K   me

- ☐ I like to work in a group because I learn from the others in my group. ☐
- ☐ When the teacher says a number, I don't understand it until I see it written. ☐
- ☐ Writing a spelling word down several times helps me remember it better. ☐
- ☐ I find it easier to remember what I have heard than what I have read. ☐
- ☐ I learn best when I study alone. ☐
- ☐ I like to listen to music, or television when I study. ☐
- ☐ If I have a choice between reading or listening, I usually listen. ☐
- ☐ I talk better than I write. ☐
- ☐ I use my hands a lot when I talk. ☐
- ☐ I can remember the pages of my homework without writing them down. ☐
- ☐ I can get more schoolwork done when I work with someone. ☐
- ☐ Written math problems are easier for me than oral. ☐
- ☐ If my homework were verbal, I would do it faster. ☐
- ☐ I study best when no one is around to talk or listen to. ☐
- ☐ I do best in classes where the information has to be read. ☐
- ☐ I like to do things with my hands, like crafts or simple repairs. ☐
- ☐ The things I write on paper seem better than when I say them. ☐
- ☐ Written assignments are easier for me. ☐
- ☐ I understand a math problem that is written better than one I hear. ☐
- ☐ I like to work by myself. ☐
- ☐ I would rather read a story, than listen to it read by someone. ☐
- ☐ I would rather show and explain how a thing works than write about it. ☐
- ☐ Saying my multiplication tables over and over helps me remember them better than writing them over and over. ☐
- ☐ I learn better by listening than by reading. ☐
- ☐ I like to make things with my hands. ☐
- ☐ I do well on tests if they are about things I hear in class. ☐

☐ It is easier when I say the numbers of a
problem to myself as I work it out. ☐
☐ I like to study with other people. ☐
☐ I like tests that call for sentence completion
or written answers. ☐
☐ I would rather tell a story than write about it. ☐

To Tally Your Score   P. 146

Score one point for every statement you marked "me". How many of those did you mark "A"? How many "V" and how many "K"?

Your highest score is your dominant sensory channel, the lowest is your least dominant channel. Write your observations and thoughts below.

While there are many differences that distinguish one culture from other cultures and society at large, there are many similarities that unite all people. Some Cultural similarities all people of the human race feel are:

Cultural Similarities

Hurt	Anger
Sadness	Fear
Loneliness	Joy
Pain	Love

Can you think of other similarities? Write them below.

Valuing Our Differences

Diversity is anything that divides us or distinguishes us from another ethnic culture or group of people. Our differences are to be understood and celebrated. Our culture can act as a bridge to bring us together as a member of the family of mankind.

Cultural Differences— Communication

P. 147

LANGUAGE (DIALECT)

Way You Process (receive) Information

1. Auditory
2. Visual
3. Kinesthetic

BODY LANGUAGE (POSTURE, MOVEMENT)

List other languages you speak or write below.

Ethnicity:

P. 148

American Indian/Alaskan Islander
Asian/Pacific Islander
Black/African American
Filipino
Hispanic
White/Caucasian
Other/Africans, Panamanian, Samoan
Puerto Rican

If your ethnic identity is not listed, please write it down.

Are you happy with your ethnicity? If your answer is no, state why below.

Political Orientation Differences

Money is seen as a means to an end, or as power.
One is not worthwhile if they cannot provide for themselves.

Values That Can Be Culturally Different are:

Cleanliness, work, family size, leisure activities, time, play
Music—Country Western, Rhythm and Blues
Humor—(quick-witted, story telling)

Ways to Communicate with Others from a Different Cultural Background
    A. Listen with the intent to hear
    B. Speak slowly P. 149
    C. Repeat statement to make sure you are heard
    D. Maintain eye contact without staring
    E. Accept the differences
    F. Practice patience
    G. Expect to learn something new

Reverend David Spears states, that "Our differences are to be accepted and celebrated".

Write down any differences you have come to accept rather than fear.

Chapter 8

How to Develop Self-Esteem in a Child   P. 151

Pride in independent thinking is the goal. Young people tend to have a strong conviction about their independence The following are positive attributes I have noticed in young people.. When parents see them they may think they are being challenged:

1. Perseverance — never giving up on what they set out to do, sticking to their purpose.
2. Determination — fixed purpose, and firmness in carrying out their purpose.
3. Ability to endure in spite of obstacles, discomfort, or pain.
4. Mental and physical ability to cope with adversity.
5. They were survivors, survive and achieve against great odds.
6. Have a goal at an early age, before the age of six.
7. Being proud of their race, and achieving as their ancestors have done in the past.
8. Showing the world their race is well rounded as a group of people.
9. Not letting their race down by failing or giving poor effort.
10. Showing the world that their race is capable of achieving, and accomplishing great things.
11. Tremendous self-determination.
12. Not letting anyone decide: who they are, who, or what they may become.

Things that block good feelings about yourself and others:

Anger
Jealousy
Resentment/Envy
Revenge
Fear/anxiety

Our good feelings (fire within us) manifest as:

P. 156

Goal→ Drive to Excel→ Energy/Vitality→
Enthusiasm→ Aliveness Light→ = Joy, Happiness, Love

Through our desires and goals we are motivated to change:

1. Identify or describe what motivates you to face each day?

2. Do you have a desire to better your circumstances or life?

3. What can you do to feel good about yourself?
   A.

   B.

4. Do you love to please or satisfy your friends, have you made a god of another human like yourself?

5. List things you can do to like yourself, or enjoy life more:

   A.

   B.

   C.

IF I RULED THE WORLD

P. 157

Let's Dream

If you could have anything you wanted, live anyplace you wanted, be anything/one you wanted, what would you ask for?

Answer The Questions Below:

1. Which famous person/s you would like to be and why?

2. In which period of time, past or future, would you choose to live, and why?

3. What foreign country would you most like to visit and why?

4. What skill/talent would you like to possess, and why?

5. What place/s in the United States would you like to visit? Why?

6. In which sport would you like to be a star, and why?

7. What kind of car would you like to own, and why?

P. 158

8. For what would you like to become famous, and why?

9. Where would you most like to live, and why?

10. What would you do with a million dollars?

11. What one change would you make if you were to become President of the United States?

12. What would you like to accomplish in your lifetime?

Changing Your World

Make some notes about each of the following questions and be ready to discuss your responses with your parents or teacher.

1. If you could change one thing in the world, what would it be? P. 161

2. How would this change your world; what would it be like then?

www.ingramcontent.com/pod-product-compliance
Lightning Source LLC
Chambersburg PA
CBHW020329130626
46549CB00003B/1095